Edition Schott

Piano · Klavier

T0077192

Nikolai Kapustin

Николай Капустин

* 1937

10 Inventions

(1993)

for Piano
für Klavier
для фортепиано

opus 73

Authorized Edition

ED 23156
ISMN 979-0-001-20786-7

www.schott-music.com

Mainz · London · Madrid · Paris · New York · Tokyo · Beijing
© 2019 Schott Music GmbH & Co. KG, Mainz · Printed in Germany

10 Inventions

opus 73

I

Nikolai Kapustin
* 1937

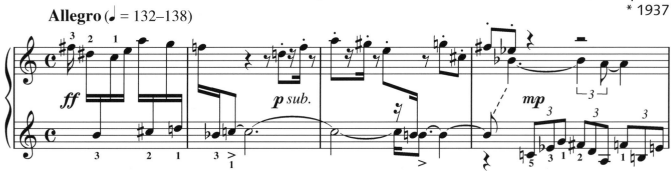

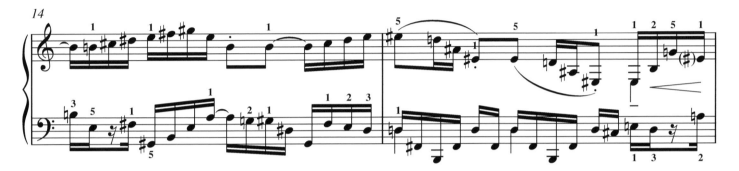

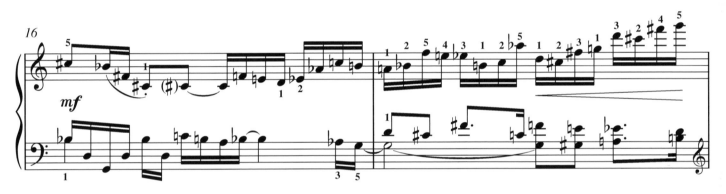

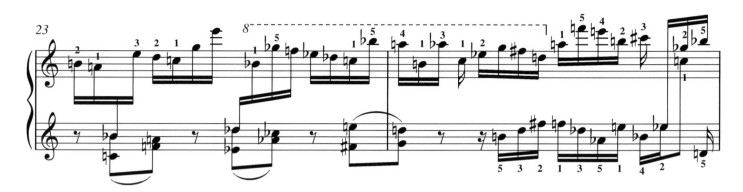

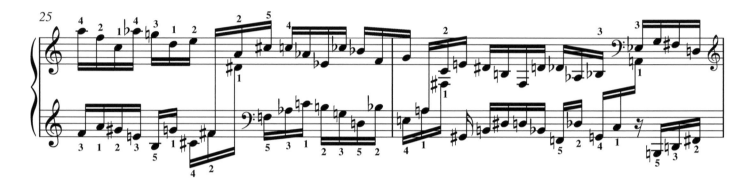

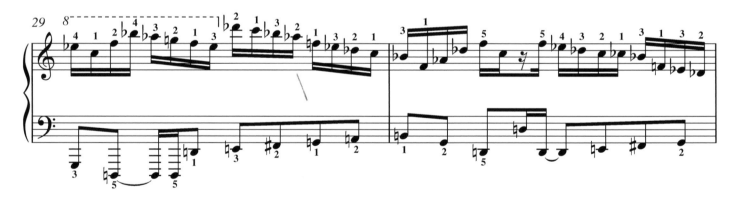

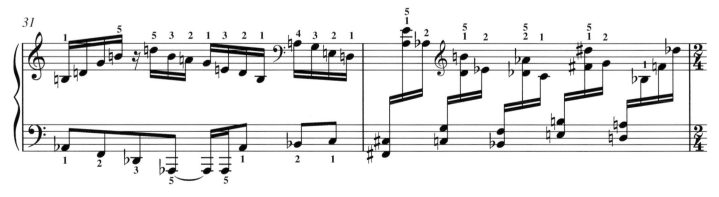

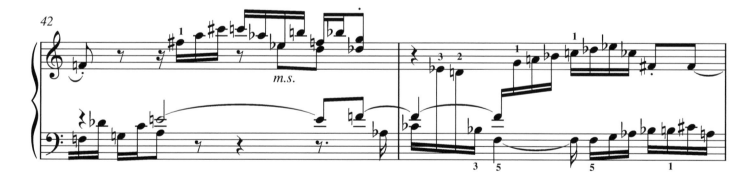

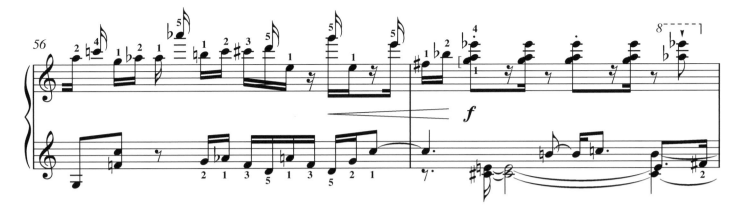

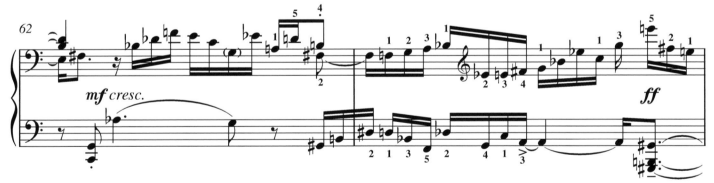

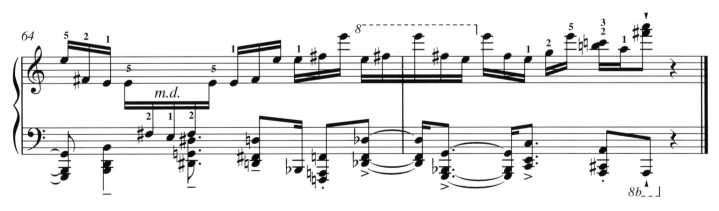

8

II

Largo (♩ = 48)

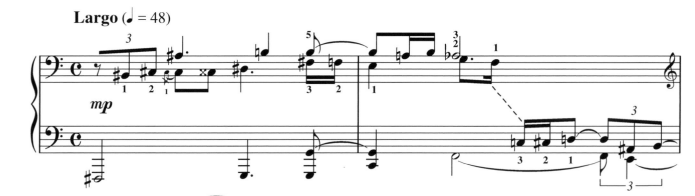

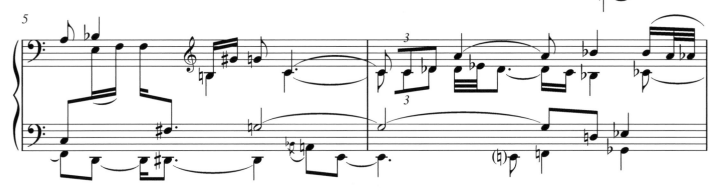

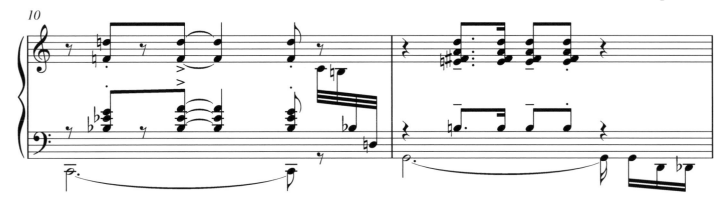

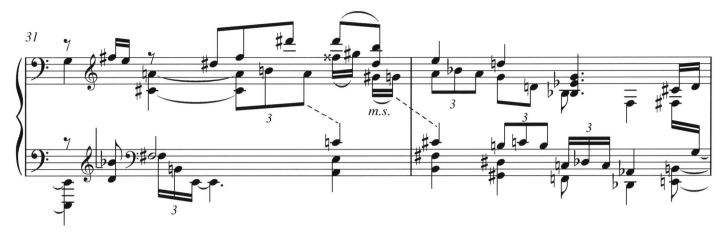

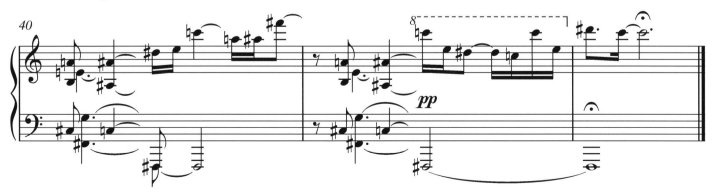

III

Allegretto giocoso (♩ = 120)

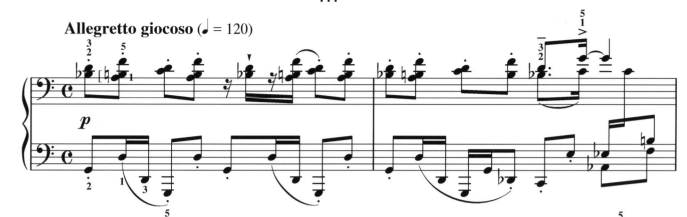

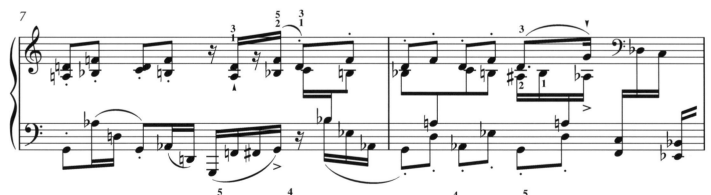

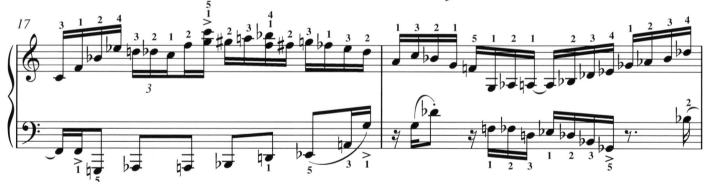

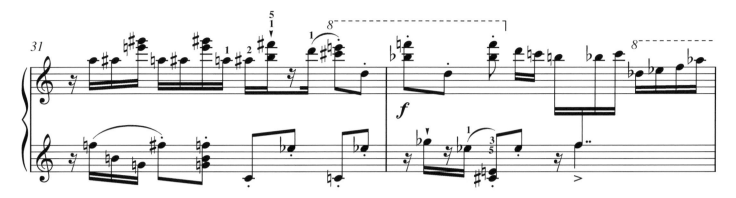

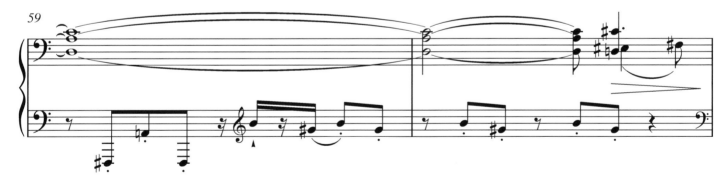

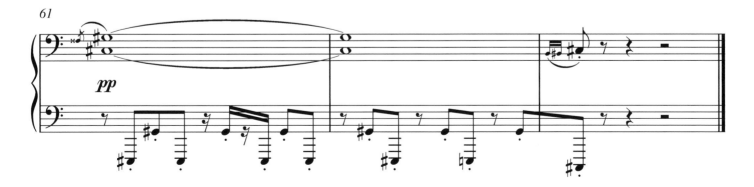

pp

IV

Allegro risoluto (♩ = 152)

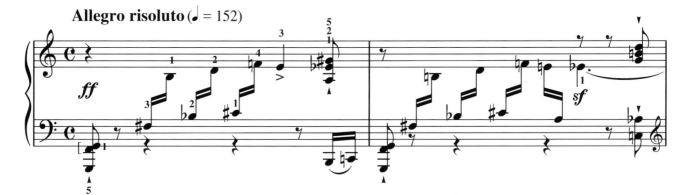

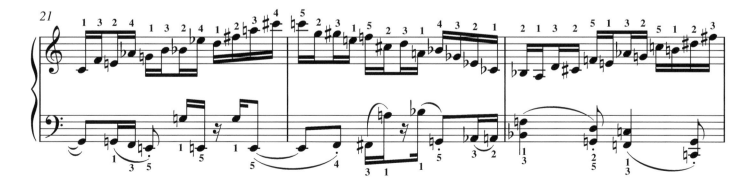

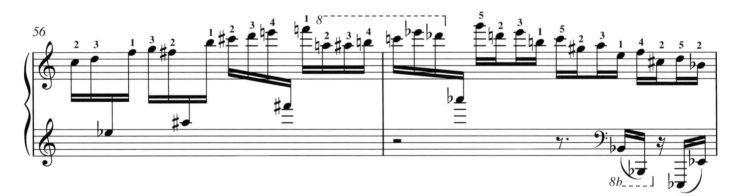

V

Grave (♩ = 42)

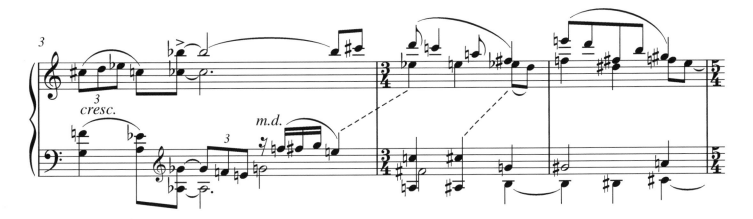

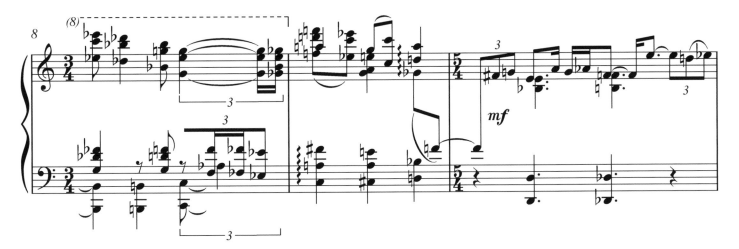

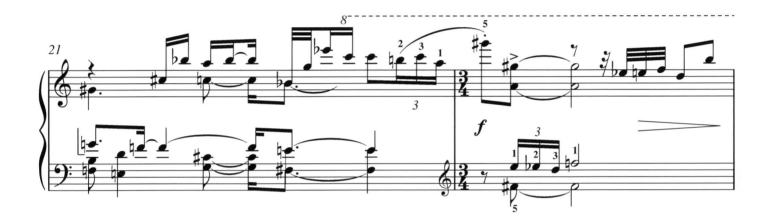

VI

Moderato

Tempo di valse ($\bullet$ = 144)

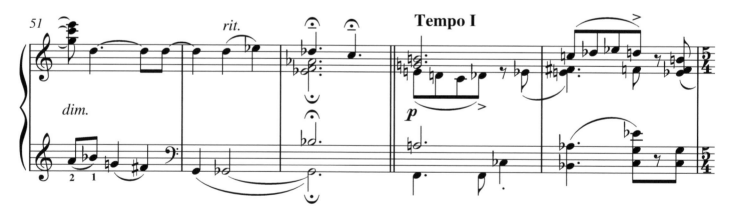

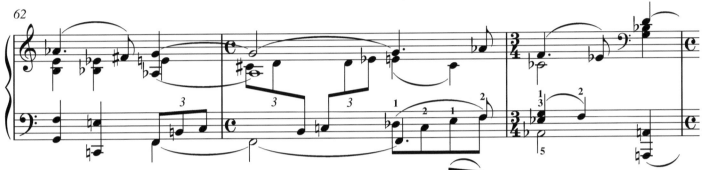

VII

Andantino ($\quarternote$ = 132)

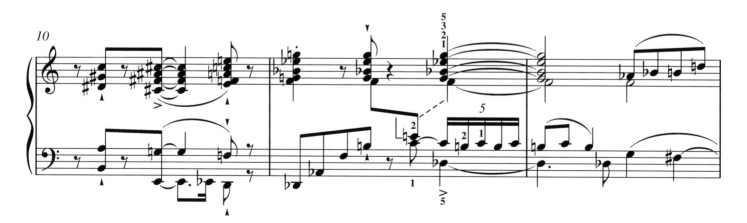

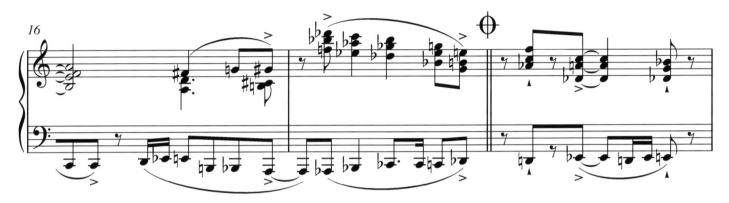

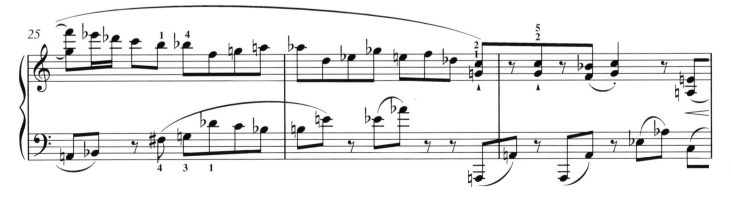

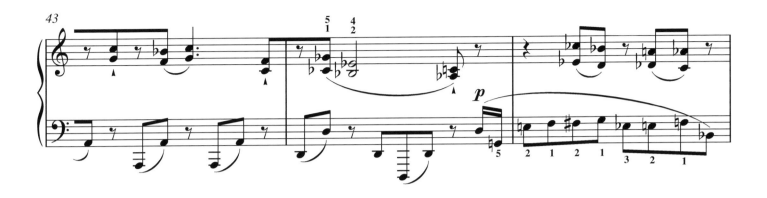

D.S. al ⊕-⊕

Coda

poco rit.

perdendosi

VIII

Feroce (♩ = 100)
sempre swinging

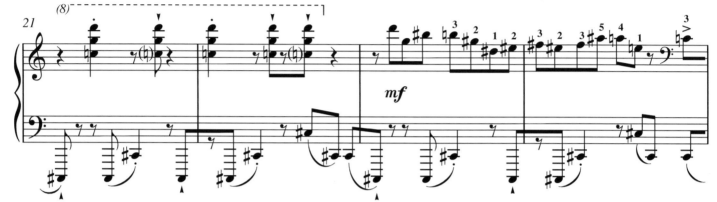

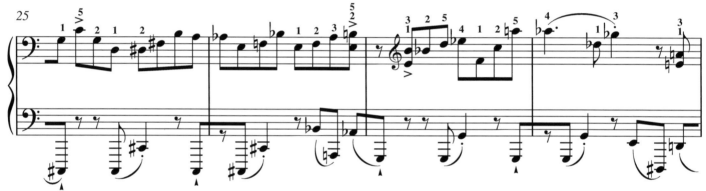

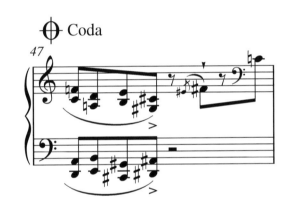

Coda

D.C. al ⊕-⊕

IX

Lento (♩ = 58)

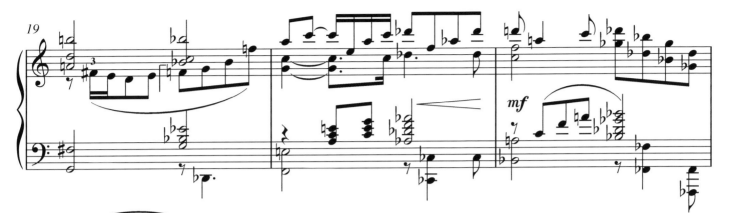

X

Vivace (= 120)

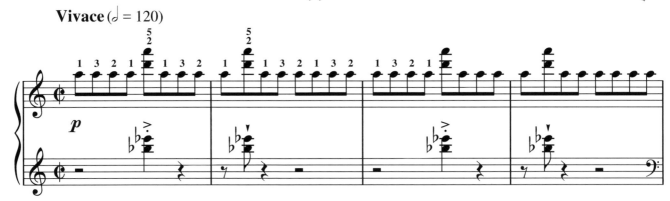

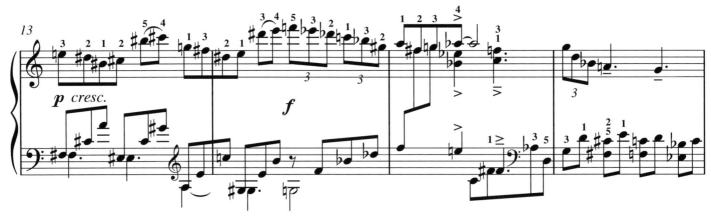

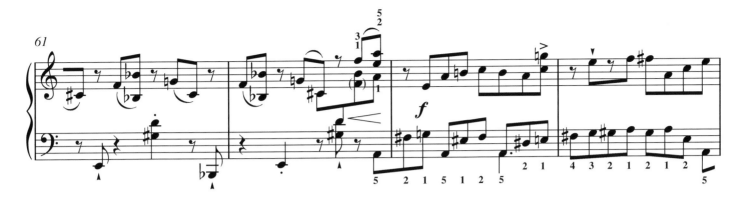

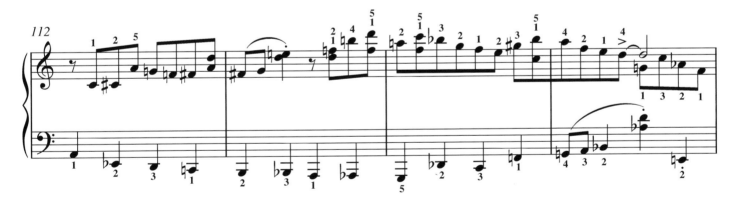